from art to ashes

CDLV, LLC

you bought me a typewriter
and told me to shine,
your love guides me
to the right words,
and your mind is forever
my favorite place to explore-

i owe this all to you.

Table of Contents

preface

homeostasis isn't perfect, but rather a flow with ups and downs,
like a wavelength. our bodies maintain balance this way-
our bodies are not perfect. throughout our lives,
we will, we have, and we continue to experience highs and lows
while struggling to maintain balance somewhere in between.
i've categorized this into two parts:
art and ashes.
these interchangeable parts are not as defined
as they are in the context of this book.
they do not have an order or a method but rather phases
that we shift through as we struggle to maintain balance.

being born in los angeles,
i never really knew how magnificent my own city was,
similar to children with famous parents.
i watched our hills catch fire from year to year
and how our scorched mountains birthed new life despite it.
i became inspired by my city's resilience
to do the same when wildfires turned my world into ashes.

everybody's art contains ashes;
that is just the nature of things.
after losing something we love,
we carry those ashes into the next chapter of our lives.

art

art

from: who i was
to: who i've become

like twin branches of the same tree,
we share a name and smell as sweet.
own how you've changed
and don't leave me in the dark,
but if you burn every page,
keep my ashes in your heart.

art

city of angels

as night approaches,
twilight hues brush against our palm trees,
before the city lights pollute the sky.

this is where larger than life
can end up homeless
and dreams have
a chance to survive.

from up here,
we can watch the traffic on the 405,
as thousands go by-
thousands taking chances
towards their dreams.

i know home becomes special
when you leave,
but i never thought
that's who i would be.

i was born and raised in this city-
this city was so normal to me,
until i listened to her
talk about her dreams.

from the 118 to the 405,
'til the 110 and back north,
she would murder for this city-
she could die feeling at home.

she's a vixen with a vintage style,
expensive taste,
and a gorgeous smile.

art

baby, you're my moulin rouge.
lotus infused,
candlelit muse-
let me take refuge.

these streets look like palm tree parades-
this is where dreams are made.
it's the city of possibilities
and most probably,
our grave.

baby girl is a hollywood
pastiche-
90's born, but her soul is from the
60's.
wildfire, but she likes to keep it
classy-
lana del rey, with a little bit of
audrey.

darling, you can have the stars,
the sky, the palm trees,
and the street lights-
honey you can have it all,
just give me one night.

night in moonlight armor,
your body is the starry sky.
your eyes, they make me wonder,
if they've ever let anything die.

she's always pushing herself to do
better than you expect her to.
it's not because she has
something to prove.
it's simply because-
fuck you.

she's my favorite piece of art
and she's covered in ashes.

the consequences were ineffable-
another visceral exchange.
our differences make us combustible,
as passion floods our pains.

we shared the worst about us,
so we could get lost
in what's left.

i can flow with the way you think
and i really love the way your ink
leaves your skin.
you're proud so it's bottled in;
i don't mind if you spill a bit.

art

you said you're feeling low,
but you've always been my high
and i know you're scared to fly,
since you've fallen from the sky.
we can take it night by night-
let me
take you
to new
heights.

22

go ahead baby,
let it out.
tell me all the things,
we couldn't talk about.

i love when you enter my veins-
i love when you replace my pain.

dim the lights
until we're silhouettes
shifting through the darkness.

falling

looking at her face,
her hair,
those lips,
they weren't mine-
she belonged to someone else.

we were parked
in a moonlit cul de sac
out of reach
of streetlights.

it was freezing,
so we shared the passenger seat.

that's when i selfishly
forsook our friendship-

i knew i couldn't go another day
without kissing her.

art

undress
and
wine down.
your heart is his,
but you're mine for now.

falling

but maybe i knew
you wanted me
as bad
     as i
did you.

i can feel the dripping,
from your petals,
running down my lips.
i can feel the passion,
in our tempo,
while gripping your hips.

falling

i felt her grip my neck,
i was waiting for a sign.
when our lips finally met,
i knew that she
                   was mine.

don't worry about your clothes
i can use my words to dress you.

let me
make your
secrets
mine.

scorch me with your burning soul;
douse me
in the oceans
of your mind.

falling

bleed into
my rifted thoughts.
watch what sprouts,
where nothing was.

art

she makes me feel like,
for a moment,
all my missing pieces
reappear.

falling

atomic muse-
you're my wick;
you're my fuse.

i could see this on you-
i can see you without it.
i would say i love you,
but you'd finesse around it.
you only need yourself
and i would never doubt it,
but baby
you may be
my only prowess.

i knew the language of her smile;
she spoke the language of my soul.

art

you never slip my imagination.
it doesn't help to see you naked-
it doesn't matter if we make it.

we explored avenues of common pleasure,
her mind is a galaxy-
                    that body is adventure.

maturity

when you embrace another's pain
as your own, just to take it away-
just so their back doesn't break,

you feel the pleasure of living for someone else.

"that's just how i am,
            for the people i love,
                        i'd do anything."

love grows with time,
but time does not dictate its age.

it takes time for most things,
but love isn't one of them.

so if you and your lover
get it right,

run with it.

art

i couldn't wait to treat you right;
you took me in
and showed me life-
and what it's like,
to get reciprocation right.

maturity

her whispers
fell on my demons,
like a guillotine.

art

this heart hasn't been broken,
since you've held it.
love is my prayer,
let me show you how i worship.

maturity

my energy leaves
like an electrical bleed
from severed links,
spilling currents.
i feel her receive-
i'm what she needs;
i let her drink,
because she loves it.

art

there wasn't a fire
that could burn
her page.

maturity

i become myself
when i'm loving you.

art

i'm in love
with your story-
where you've been
and where you're going.

maturity

you've become
my rain and shine;
you decompress
my mind.

art

one of a kind-
but what makes you amazing
is the way you feel the same
when i think that i'm crazy.

maturity

till our home becomes walls
and dust turns to stars,
i love you.

between these lines/
you & i/
forever.

maturity

in a different sequence of events,
if you and i had never met,
if i could revisit mistakes and regrets,
and twist together all the ends.
from who i've loved
to who you left,
if it was possible to circumvent-
i wouldn't.

and so we loved away our happy ending
and burned along with all our bindings.

maturity

one more time/
before you leave/
make me feel home.

the void

the void is the end of the tunnel,
the reason behind your fears-

that nothing in this life will last,
we are destined to return to ashes.

all that will remain
is the love
we've left behind.

the void is death-
the end

that will leave spaces in the hearts of others,
as others have left in yours.

all things living
will struggle to comprehend this truth

because the void is an ugly truth

and that makes it all beautiful.

ashes

when a soul is pushed
beyond what it can take,
and a heart can no longer endure
the burden of its aches-
it breaks.

a broken heart
whispers two truths about a person,
how they have loved and
how they will love.

her heart mourns for moments
she knew would never last,
but instead of being buried by her past,
she became the beauty
covered in ashes.

destruction

the violent red sky and murk-
a painful reminder that
everything still burns.

our love, our nights,
and all those laughs-
up in flames.

we are both to blame
for the blood that flows
down the LA river-

too many people got involved.

too many people
for nothing resolved,
but we never learned.

fighting fire with fire
nothing was left
unburnt.

ashes

you'd have me reduced to nothing-
you'd rather that,
than feel something.

destruction

the more you call me destructive,
the more i'll keep to my ways.
the more you love me,
the more i'll push you away.

it's a storm
brewing in my chest,
a demon
digging its roots
into my soul.
i could feel
my skin lose its warmth-
i can feel
my heart grow cold
and i let it.

destruction

fuck your shit.

but baby it's okay-
these are things i'm used to.
i know you can't be changed-
that's why i lied too.
i didn't mean it
when i said
i love you.

yesterday you had
a different reason,
today you say that
i'm out of control.
everything i do,
you treat like treason-
tomorrow you'll pretend
you didn't know.

ashes

it's not that i don't think about you;
of course i miss you baby.
it's just-
you're cancerous.

destruction

heartbreak blurs our interactions;
what is left is just a fraction.
i miss when all your words were actions-
i miss a time that heart held passion.

ashes

i'm the happiest
when i can't tell
if i'm lying
to myself.

destruction

i know you need a reply,
but all i've got is nonchalance.
the only way to move on was
to starve you of a response.

you were so romantic
when i was someone you needed,
but now i'm treated
like the rest of your toys-
depleted and defeated.

destruction

i've heard apologies,
i've tried new beginnings,
and now-
i'm tired of starting over.

with stillness in silence

ashes of our past
descend from the sky.

it's both eerie and ironic,
watching the aftermath
of such an unforgiving wrath
fall so gently,

covering everything
including me-

i watch with stillness
in silence.

beautifully slow,
it falls to the floor,
imitating snow.
the skies filled with the murky glow
of burning homes reduced to smoke.
some fled in cars and some on all fours,
but not a soul could change the pace
of nature and her ruthless force.

the weight of our love
burst into flames on my skin,
burning seconds into hours,
and months into years,
until the ashes fit in my palm.

i've paid my dues,
i don't owe you a thing.
i don't owe you a ring-
through means through.

unlike you,
i'm not afraid
to take responsibility.
most things tend
to end in flames,
the rest i've burned
myself.

fighting the urge to raise my voice,
i swallowed the passion in my heart.
you mistook the fire in my eyes;
you couldn't tell the love apart-
it wasn't violence,
but kindness,
that left you in the dark.

well maybe
we burn to see what's left
when all our walls come down
and maybe
we need to break to learn
to build them back up.
well baby
how do you think i feel
to see you calling now–
when you've acted like
there was nothing left
of our love.

maybe you would listen;
maybe we could talk
without
the static interference.

i'd hate to see you cry
as the result
of my decisions,

but for now
i can't afford
another
this time will be different.

mind your own life,
i don't need you to help.
i don't want your advice,
i'm hard enough on myself.

it hurts to see
a day i've seen
a thousand times,
but i can't seem
to break from this
routine.
i know if i let go
i'll clear space in my mind,
but losing you
has been far from easy.

you saved your feelings
for a single text
you probably reread,
six times,
before you pressed send.

and now,
you need a friend.

with plenty to say,
i didn't engage.
i did not burst into flames,
rage, or curse your name.
i sought solace in change,
making everyone believe
i have grown patient and tamed.
knowing full well my words
would never hold weight,
i planned to kill you with-

too late.

i'm sure you don't remember,

when everybody left you
and i told you i never would.

i promise you'll do better-
no doubt that you'll do better.

it just won't be

me.

ashes

then let me sit with
what remains of our ashes,
just a bit longer.

understanding

it has been so long since
i have looked at myself in the mirror,
i have aged.

more than a few details in my face-
my expressions have changed.

how have i become this way?

i couldn't blame it on you
and that was most terrifying truth-

why do we do the things we do?

can't you see i'm hurting too?

i know what you've been through-
at least,

i understand you.

ashes

when you left
a part of me died-
a part that didn't deserve it.
when you left
i realized-
i realized nobody's perfect.

understanding

her mind was clouded
because she needed closure
and it wasn't there.

you have let your pain
turn you into a monster,
but i understand.

understanding

too busy saving face
to notice the mess you've made.
a victim of shame,
but far from unusual.
let's see who you'll blame
when your blessings
aren't fruitful.

the mountains you claim
to have climbed on your own,
came at a price
that was never paid.
even the reddest rose
will wither and fade,
drinking alone
from a broken vase.

understanding

you love to talk about moving on,
but act stuck
in the same position.

immersed in an ocean of misery,
drowning beneath the surface,
and gasping for moments of relief.
your heavy heart did not sink,
it plunged,
deep into your fears and insecurities,
until you finally couldn't breathe.

but then you reached-
but then you stood on your feet.

understanding

you swear you're off the deep end,
but you surface kind of frequent.

ashes

she knew you would say
all that needed to be said,
by hesitating.

understanding

you can fool yourself,
but you cannot lie to me.
i've been you, baby.

ashes

i finally get it, you're this way
because you needed to change-
because staying the same
cost you everything.

understanding

when you feel the world is ending,
but it's the start of the day

and you're walking on eggshells,
but haven't made a mistake.

when you need to take a break
before you go to wash your face-

turn the page.

rebirth

it doesn't always
happen on its own,
sometimes it's a decision-
a choice you have to make
despite the odds.

be brave.

where mountains have burned,
flowers have bloomed.
if they can defy destruction,
so can you.

like a phoenix out of misery,
i'm reborn when you're
the death of me.

don't tell me who you used to be,
show me who you are.

fuck your potential,
this is my potential.

rebirth

i hope my name rattles your spine,
i bet you wish that you were mine.

ashes

i was searching my heart
for a place i couldn't find,
until i realized,
home is where you
start your new life.

rebirth

be stunning
be strange
don't be afraid
    to feel complete.

ashes

my mind is clear
and my heart's in bloom,
i'm ready to try
           something new.

rebirth

the moon will still rise,
after everything you love
has become ashes.

judging from the past,
nothing can last forever,
but maybe this will.

tragedy is responsible
for my most beautiful beginnings.

dedication

we spent a lazy sunday morning at a typical LA cafe
where they ask a question of the day.
the server asked,
"how do you plan to leave your footprint on this planet."
it was as though you knew the end of her sentence
because before she could finish,
you pointed at me
and said,
i have two of them.

"i always get so emotional, why don't you cry when you get sad?"
"i used to be that way, but i learned to control it."
"and if i can't control it?"
"then don't."

you protected me from how the world is
by letting me live in your love.
i thought i wouldn't be strong enough,
until i understood how selfish that was.

i felt the power of your passion-
you made me feel good enough.
i understood the magnitude of your strength,
in the absence of your love.

dad, thank you.

"more than there are stars in the sky."
you'd tell me how much you loved me every night.

we really had it all back then,
at least, that's how you made it feel.

things between us had always been crazy,
but without dad to help sort things out-
i'm sorry.

there is a lot you and i are still getting right,
but without you i wouldn't have this life.
you taught me to believe in myself-
to stand up
to fight.

i think about you every night.

thank you mom, i love you.

you are the first best friend i ever had,
even though we bump heads,
you remind me of dad.
he's in your smile
he's in your laugh.

"allen,
look at me,
i promise you,
we're going to make it."

without your ambitions
to compliment my dreams
or your crazy
to fuel my madness
i wouldn't be
me.

my brother, best friend,
and confidant.

i love you.

Made in the USA
Las Vegas, NV
31 August 2021